KU-771-546

Guides enjoying a camp fire chorus

Membership of the Guide Movement breaks through all barriers between nationalities, colour, class and religious creed.

It also breaks through the barriers created by disability, for the fact that a girl cannot see, cannot hear, cannot walk, need not stop her from becoming a Guide.

Even distance is no barrier, for a girl in remote parts can join in Guide Meetings and Patrol Meetings by post.

To become a member of the Guide Movement is to join a great worldwide family, and friendships made will be friendships for life.

This book will tell you just what Guiding is all about.

Acknowledgments
The author and publishers wish to thank the Girl Guides Association for their help in the preparation of this book.
Acknowledgment is also made of additional photographs and illustrative material: pages 17, 21, 23, 24, 34 and 35 – Tim Clark; pages 8, 9, 12, 13, 14, 22, 47 and 51 – Girl Guides Association; page 45, Christopher Reed; page 11, B H Robinson.

© LADYBIRD BOOKS LTD MCMLXXX

All rights reserved. No part of this publication may be reproduced, stored in a retrieval system, or transmitted in any form or by any means, electronic, mechanical, photocopying, recording or otherwise, without the prior consent of the copyright owner.

Shelagh Anderson

GIRL GUIDES

by NANCY SCOTT
photographed by JOHN MOYES

Ladybird Books Loughborough

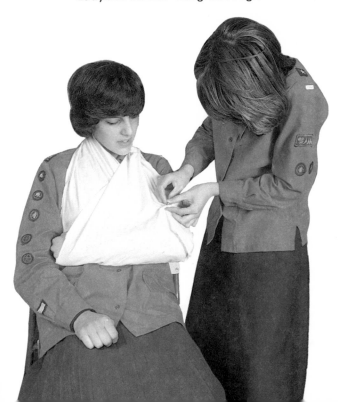

What is a Guide? If you have been a Brownie Guide, you may answer that a Guide is a girl who is over the age of ten to eleven years and so cannot stay in the Brownie Pack after her eleventh birthday, but must go on to the Guide Company.

That is part of the answer, of course. But a Guide does not need to have been a Brownie Guide first. Any girl over ten years of age, and under fifteen years, can become a Guide – provided she is willing to make the Promise that all Guides and Scouts make.

It is the Promise which makes Guiding and Scouting a special kind of youth group. The Promise gives its members a purpose in life, a way to follow. But more about the Promise later.

First, let us look at some of the things Guides DO.

They get out of doors as much as possible, because there are so many opportunities for fun and adventure out of doors.

They explore – their own neighbourhood and further afield; they hike; they cook out of doors; they cycle; they follow maps in orienteering games; they follow the tracks of wild creatures and observe how they live in their natural habitats; they play games of all kinds; they climb; they swim; they visit historic buildings; they explore ancient churches;

they camp... Guides love going to places and finding out about things.

Tracking a fox

To enjoy all these things to the full, however, they have first to learn about the right clothes to wear, how to light a cooking fire, how to read a map, where wild creatures are to be found, how to climb a mountain safely, how to swim proficiently, and where the interesting and historic buildings and churches are to be found.

And to do all these things well, they must be fit, so Guides discover how to keep themselves healthy.

They know how to help other people in times of danger or accident by learning many of the skills required in first aid and home nursing.

Practising first aid

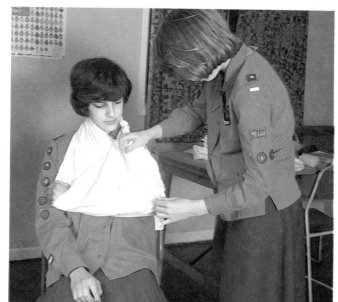

Learning how to read a map

Guides are friendly people. They make many new friends, not only in their own Patrol and Company, but by meeting Guides from other Companies, and corresponding with Guide pen-friends overseas. Their friendship goes beyond their own circle – to old people, to handicapped people, to children in Homes, to lonely people.

Guides enjoy creating things; drawing, painting, modelling, carving, writing, dancing, singing, acting, knitting, sewing. They give concerts and stage plays; help at bazaars and fêtes. There are so many ways Guides use their creative hands, for their own pleasure and to give pleasure and help to others.

Lord Baden-Powell, founder of the Boy Scout and Girl Guide Movements

But why are they called Guides? How did they get this name?

Brownie Guides already know that the Scouting and Guiding Movement was started by Robert Baden-Powell, and you can read more about this great man and his life in the Ladybird Brownie Guides, Cub Scouts and Scouts books.

Scouting began first, but soon girls wanted to be members of the exciting new club. So they formed their own groups, calling themselves Girl Scouts. But at the beginning of the twentieth century when Scouts began, it was not considered ladylike for girls to do many of the vigorous and active things the boys were allowed to do.

Now Robert Baden-Powell, being an extremely wise man, knew that if the girls continued copying the boys in everything they did, it would not only annoy the boys, but it would also annoy the grown-ups. This might well result in the girls being forbidden entirely to join the new Girl Scout groups, and might even damage the reputation of the fast-growing Scout Movement.

So he decided to form a Movement specially for the girls. He included in it many of the adventurous active things the boys did, but also certain skills of which girls were then expected to have a sound knowledge – skills to do with making and looking after a home.

It's great fun toffee making!

He called this new Movement the Girl Guides, taking the word 'Guide' from two sources. The first was from a famous corps of Guides in India who were men known for their general hardiness, their resourcefulness in dealing with difficult situations, their keenness and their courage. They were a force trained to take up any duties required of them, and to turn their hands to anything.

The second source was from the mountaineering guides in Switzerland, and other mountainous regions. These are men who can guide people over the most difficult and dangerous parts with bravery and skill; men who can rescue and help those in trouble; men who enjoy the excitement that life in a difficult and often dangerous region presents.

So, said Robert Baden-Powell, the word 'Guide' had come to mean one who possesses all these good qualities, including industry, common sense, and self-reliance.

It is all these qualities that Guides down the years have tried to gain through an interesting programme of training and service to others.

At first the girls, who already called themselves Girl Scouts, were not at all keen on the change of name, nor the change in the programme. They preferred to be SCOUTS, and to keep their strong

Some of the first Girl Guides

Patrol names. To many of them it seemed a great come-down to change from membership of the Lion or Kangaroo Patrol to being Poppies or Lilies-of-the-Valley! And they much preferred boys' pursuits to those considered suitable for girls.

Then when they understood why such changes were necessary, they soon got over their disgruntled feelings, and threw themselves with even greater enthusiasm into Guiding as it continued to grow and grow at a rapid pace.

The Guide and Scout Movement began in Great Britain, but such a grand game as Guiding could not be kept to one country alone. The girls of other countries began to hear about Guiding and wanted to become members.

The United States was one of the first countries outside Britain to take it up. Mrs Juliette Low, a friend of Baden-Powell, was one of the early pioneers of Guiding and Scouting. She had already started several companies in Great Britain before returning to her native town Savannah in the state of Georgia, USA, in 1912. There she immediately gathered together a group of girls and told them about the

Guides in Britain; soon these girls were clamouring for a troop of their own. So Juliette Low made what has since become known as her 'famous phone call', to a friend, saying: "Come right over. I have got something for the girls of Savannah, and all America, and all the world, and we are going to begin tonight."

Mrs Juliette Low

How right she was! From thousands in Britain, the Movement grew to several million throughout the world, and in 1928 the big Guide family officially took the name 'The World Association of Girl Guides and Girl Scouts'. In some countries, as for example The United States of America, they prefer to keep the earlier name of Girl Scouts.

After her marriage in 1912 to Sir Robert Baden-Powell (as he was then), Olave, Lady Baden-Powell, helped her husband with the early organisation of the Girl Guides. She was made Chief Guide in 1918, and World Chief Guide in 1930, a position which she held until her death in 1977.

English and Norwegian Guides at an international camp in North Yorkshire

Although there are differences in the uniforms worn throughout the world, yet all members of the World Association have a motto, many sharing the same one – 'Be Prepared'; all greet each other with the same sign or salute with three raised fingers, which reminds all Guides of their Promise; all wear the trefoil in the Promise Badge; all use the left handshake of friendship; and all overcome the barriers of language between different nationalities with a smile. Any Guide who has attended a World Camp or Conference will tell you how valuable these shared signs and a wide, warm smile can be in bridging the gap between the races and creating a friendly family feeling.

Although from all these outward signs you can tell they are all members of the same big family of Guiding, these are just the outward signs and symbols. The strength of Guiding lies inwards, in the Promise which all Guides and Girl Scouts make, and do their best to keep.

The Promise presents a high ideal to live up to; it is a challenge. And every girl who becomes a Guide accepts this challenge, knowing that she is not alone in trying to do her best to live up to the high standard set, for she has a great world wide family of friends to support and encourage her.

So, what is this Promise that makes the family of Guiding such a special kind of youth group?

The actual words of the Promise vary a little between one country and another, but their meaning and spirit are the same. All put service to God first, then service to one's country, and to one's fellow-man, and finally a clause promising to try to keep the Guide Law.

Every Guide who makes this Promise is *trusted* to do her best to keep it. The words 'do her best' are very important. No one expects that the moment a girl makes the Promise she at once becomes a paragon of virtue! But she promises *to do her best* in all she says, does, and thinks – not just when she is in uniform, or at a Guide Meeting or other Guide function, but every day, everywhere.

The Guide Law makes ten positive statements. It does not say what a Guide may be, or can be, or should be – it states what she *is*.

This is the Law:

1 A Guide is loyal and can be trusted.

2 A Guide is helpful.

3 A Guide is polite and considerate.

4 A Guide is friendly and a sister to all Guides.

5 A Guide is kind to animals and respects all living things.

6 A Guide is obedient.

7 A Guide has courage and is cheerful in all difficulties.

8 A Guide makes good use of her time.

9   A Guide takes care of her own possessions and those of other people.

10 A Guide is self-controlled in all she thinks, says, and does.

So this is the serious idea behind all the fun, adventure and the excitement of Guiding – this is the foundation.

The Promise Badge, its trefoil symbolising the three-fold Promise

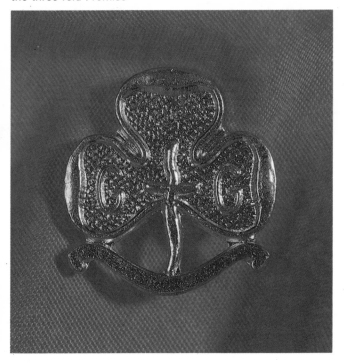

A new member meets her Patrol

Guides and Scouts share a motto — BE PREPARED, and much of the programme followed in Guide Meetings and activities is aimed at preparing Guides to meet the many challenges and emergencies of life, so that they will positively 'be prepared' physically and mentally.

But let's get back to the beginning again — to the first Guide Meeting a new member attends. If she has been a Brownie Guide, then she will be used to playing games, and doing many things with a small group of Brownies called a Six. But if she is altogether new to Guiding, she may be very puzzled indeed when the Guider in charge says something like this: 'Oh, you will be in the Cornflower Patrol with Jean,' or 'The Wren Patrol are waiting to welcome you.' She will soon discover however that 'going into' a Patrol is something very special in Guiding and Scouting.

A newcomer is shown the Patrol equipment

All Guide Companies are made up of a number of Patrols. A Patrol is a small group of from four to eight Guides, with a Patrol Leader chosen by the members of that Patrol, and a Patrol Second who is chosen by the Leader.

Most of the Guiding activities a Guide takes part in will be done in her own Patrol, and the success of a Patrol depends on each individual member of it. A successful Patrol is one in which every member shares fully in its work and in its play. In fact − where every member 'does her best' to make her Patrol the busiest and the happiest group possible.

Patrols are usually called after birds or flowers, or trees. In long-established Companies, such names are rarely changed because they have become traditional and have many 'Old Guides' linked to them.

In many cases, trophies won by the Patrol in the past will be inscribed with their name, colours and emblems. But a new Company sometimes likes to be up-to-date and invent new names for its Patrols, and it is free to do so, provided the names chosen are inspiring and attractive, and also have some lasting value. Since a Guide wears the emblem of her Patrol on the left-hand side of her uniform, the name of a new Patrol must be one which can be well illustrated on the size of badge worn.

Every group of people, large or small, must have a leader – someone in authority – otherwise there is chaos and nothing gets done. So every Patrol has a Patrol Leader, whose job it is to help the rest of the Patrol to carry out its chosen activities.

She has to encourage and help all the members in their Guiding progress, and to make sure that Guiding in her Patrol is challenging and fun for everyone. She also represents the Patrol at the Patrol Leaders' Council.

The Patrol Second is chosen by the Patrol Leader, and her job is to assist the Leader in every way she can, and also to take over the leadership of the Patrol should the Leader be away at any time.

A good Leader will arrange for other members of the Patrol to do certain jobs, rather than try to do everything herself. For instance, if the Patrol decides to keep a Log Book of the Patrol's activities and achievements, then someone will be appointed Secretary.

The Patrol Secretary will then be responsible for writing up the Log Book, or she may ask other members of the Patrol to write items to go in it. She will also write any Patrol letters that may be necessary.

Guides run a Jumble Sale

A Patrol member who is good at drawing and painting will become the Patrol artist, illustrating the Log Book; decorating the equipment and notepaper, etc. Another Patrol member may be appointed Treasurer. Her job will be to collect and record the money that the Patrol members contribute to Patrol funds. A busy, active Patrol often finds that it needs extra money from time to time.

All Guides pay a regular subscription to *Company Funds*. This money is used to finance the Company and pay for equipment. A part of every Guide's weekly subscription goes to Guide Commonwealth Headquarters, because like all big organisations, there are many heavy and regular expenses to be met.

Regular subscriptions to Company funds and to Patrol Funds however are often not enough to meet

the needs of a lively Company, and so ways to raise more money have to be found.

When knights of olden times went out on their missions, they were ordered to be thrifty, and to earn money when they needed it, instead of being a burden to others. They also earned money to give away to those in need. Baden-Powell believed that this was a good way, and that Guides and Scouts should follow it.

Earning money can be fun especially if everyone in the Patrol, and in the Company, does her bit.

If money is needed quickly, then a Jumble Sale is the easiest to organise. A Bring-and-Buy Sale can be combined with a Coffee Evening, or Morning, and a short entertainment, which will also give an opportunity for certain Guides to qualify for the Hostess Badge, and others to qualify for an Entertainer's Badge.

A Christmas Bazaar or a Spring Fair can be great fun to work for. They give a chance for all manner of skills to be put into practice: doll-dressing, toy-making, sweet-making, cakes and jams, boxes of seedlings, bowls of bulbs, pot-plants of all kinds. A wide-awake Company, discussing and pooling their ideas, can think up many novelty stalls to add to the attraction of the Sale.

Long-term money-making schemes – often needing sympathetic parents who can provide storage space – are money-back bottles, newspapers, wool-waste, used stamps, and metal foil. Such collecting schemes are often much easier to organise in a Patrol than in the Company as a whole. Every Patrol member pledges herself to bring a few newspapers, or a bag of *clean* milk-bottle tops, every week, and hands them to a Patrol Collector.

Collecting stamps for a Blue Peter appeal

Not only do Guides earn money for their own needs but, remembering the knights of old, they seek to earn and save money to help people less fortunate than themselves, in their own country, and in other countries where so much help is needed.

A Company may decide to help a local cause or, through the Girl Guide Friendship Fund, they may help in a much larger and wider project.

One such project was called 'Saving Sight', and arose from the medical discovery that the cause of so much distressing blindness in Indian babies was a Vitamin A deficiency. Vitamin A is in green vegetables, but green vegetables are scarce in parts of India, and so is money. Yet just one cupful of green vegetables taken every day would both prevent and cure this blindness. Where was the money to come from to buy the vegetables? An appeal was launched through the Guide and Brownie magazines, asking for £5000.

Within a few months not only had the £5000 been raised by the Guides and Brownies, but they had doubled that figure – £10000! And the ways in which some of the money was raised were quite remarkable, even amusing – and must have been great fun, too. For instance, can you imagine the number of shells that had first to be collected, then washed and sorted, to make 255 perfect shell mice? Can you walk on stilts? One Patrol mastered this particularly difficult balancing art, and held a sponsored Stilt-walk in an empty car park.

Making Christmas cards for sale in aid of Company funds

Another Company held a sponsored Knit-in. First they collected oddments of wool, then at the Knit-in itself, they knitted as many equal sized squares as they could within a given time. This involved many Challenges – collecting enough wool, getting willing sponsors, and then practising knitting skills until they became really proficient. Afterwards the squares were sewn together to make warm blankets for elderly people.

But everything a Guide does, comes back to the importance of the Patrol in the first place, for nearly all schemes are evolved first in Patrol Meetings.

A Patrol not only meets at the weekly Company Meetings, but tries to hold its own meetings regularly. These are the greatest fun of all, because then the members themselves choose what they want to do, how to do it, and where they want to go.

Collecting milk-bottle tops for charity

Even if a Patrol is unable to meet together regularly, apart from the weekly Company Meeting, a Guide need never be at a loss for something interesting and worthwhile to do. She only has to explore the pages of her own Guide Handbook to find numerous ideas and suggestions for challenging and interesting things she can tackle, all aimed at developing her skill and knowledge.

Guides and Brownies entertain the elderly at a Christmas party

The activities a Patrol plans on its own often depend on where the members are able to hold their meetings, and on the weather and time of year. In-door meetings, and winter meetings, are grand times to become super-proficient at certain handcraft skills, such as soft toy-making. This could be combined with a special Good Turn by giving the toys made to a local children's home or hospital.

Or the Patrol may decide to get up a short Concert to entertain the elderly people of a senior citizens club or retirement home.

Even in winter it is possible to hold Patrol meetings outdoors by planning a Patrol hike to a place of particular interest such as an old church or disused railway cutting (a splendid place for nature study). The Patrol could climb a particularly high hill to note the lie of the land around, to sketch it, or to photograph it. The hike can also help to develop skill in map and compass-reading. A great deal of ground can be covered on a winter hike, because it is necessary to keep on the move in cold weather. And landmarks are more obvious when the trees and bushes are bare.

A summer hike can combine stalking, and hike-fire cooking.

Lighting a fire in winter

An outdoor meeting in a garden or park is a good chance to practise running, jumping, ball-throwing, rope-throwing, in preparation for the Agility Badge test.

A Patrol, always keeping in mind the importance of giving service to others, might plan to tidy the garden of an elderly, sick or infirm person.

In fact there is no end to the things a Patrol can do together, provided they really plan their time.

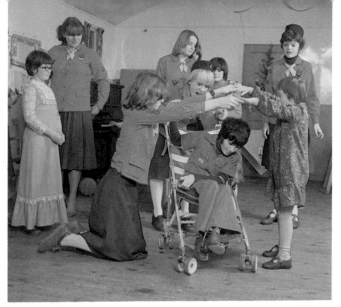
Guides hold a Christmas party for local handicapped children

Although it is nice just to sit and chat together sometimes, a Guide knows that after a time continuous idle chatter achieves nothing, it only leads to the cry, 'We don't DO anything!' And people who don't DO anything soon become bored and drift apart.

Guides are never bored, because they are always busy doing something . . . something to help others; something to develop their own personal skill and ability, so making them better able to give service; something to keep their minds and bodies fit and healthy.

Badges By now you will have noticed that Gui
wear many badges on their uniform.
All the badges worn have special
meaning and purpose.

Some are the insignia of a
Guide's membership − the
Promise Badge *(see page 17)*;
the title tape, showing the
name of her Company; the
County Badge on the point of
her tie; her Patrol Emblem. The

Patro

other badges show her progress in Guiding.

For example, do you see the small
yellow trefoil-shaped badge
above the Patrol Emblem? That is
a First Year Eight Point Badge.

Eight P

It shows that this Guide has completed a full y
as a Guide, and during that time has made real p
gress in all she has done . . . by herself, with
Patrol, and with her Company.

The twelve-monthly Eight Point badges − yel
for first year, green for second, red for third, blue
fourth − are the most important badges, beca
they show that a Guide is becoming more and m
able to carry out the meaning of her Promise.

Badges
in place

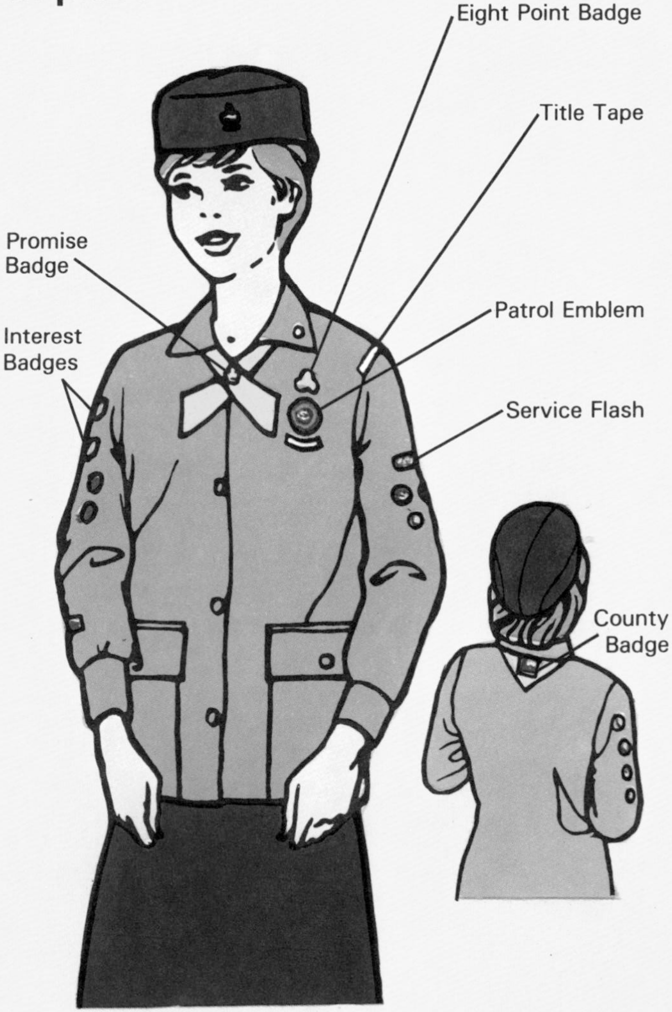

Eight Point Badge

Title Tape

Promise
Badge

Interest
Badges

Patrol Emblem

Service Flash

County
Badge

In addition to these, a Guide may gain several Interest Badges. These are called *Interest* badges, because the name says exactly what they are — the subjects in which a Guide is particularly interested. So a Guide who is a keen dancer can learn more about the art and improve her performance in order to qualify for Dancers' Badge. Or maybe she is particularly interested in wild life, so she will discover more about the fascinating and secret lives of animals, learn how she can protect them, and qualify for Bird Watcher or Naturalist Badge.

But perhaps a Guide wishes to discover fresh and exciting hobbies to follow, so she will then use her Guide Handbook to find new and challenging Interest Badges she can tackle, such as Fire Fighter, Map Reader, Artist, Boatswain, Accident Prevention, Friend to Deaf People, Horsewoman, Music Lover, Skater, Skier, Photographer, Gymnast, Gardener, Entertainer, Reader, Writer — there seems no end to them.

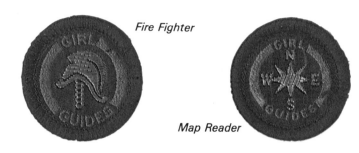

Fire Fighter

Map Reader

A Guide can begin working for an Interest Badge as soon as she becomes a Guide, and the Badges can be worn throughout her time in the Company.

There are some badges, however, which are called Service Badges, and a Guide must retake these after two years, or she loses the badge. These Badges call for a very high standard in service for others, and include such subjects as First Aid, Home Nursing, Emergency Helper, Life Saver and Rescuer.

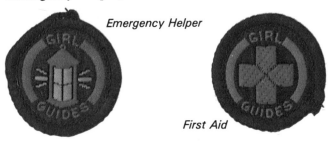

Emergency Helper

First Aid

Yet another badge a Guide can achieve, and be proud to wear, is the Service Flash. This is awarded to a Guide who has given continual personal service to an individual, or to a community for no less than four months on end, or has spent at least forty hours in a year doing many acts of service for others. This badge also must be renewed within two years, or be forfeited.

Service Flash

*This is a Patrol Enterprise Pennant, and
can be earned by a Patrol which has
suggested and carried out a really worthwhile
enterprise*

Yes, there is so much to do in Guiding, which is
grand. But, of course, it also has its dangers. With so
many ideas presented there is always the danger
that – 'being spoilt for choice' – a Guide may chop
and change too often, just nibbling at ideas, and
never completing anything properly. So to help a
Patrol which is in danger of drifting into this 'nibbling and achieving nothing' attitude, there are
special challenges a Patrol can train for if they wish.
When they pass the challenges set, they are then
awarded Pennants, known as Patrol Interest Pennants.

Of course these Pennants are only awarded to a
Patrol whose members have really worked together,
and achieved a high standard in all they have done.

This can only come through much thought and careful planning on the part of the Patrol. Yet it is not nearly such a daunting project as it may appear at first sight, because the whole Patrol works together, making use of each Guide's own special ability, from the newest member to the experienced Patrol Leader.

Pennants present a fascinating range of activities, from exploration of the course of an ancient trackway or river, to amusing a small child with handmade toys; from cooking a meal for the whole Patrol on an outdoor hike fire, to preparing and presenting a complete Camp Fire programme; from transmitting messages over a long distance by varying methods, to making woodcraft gadgets for use in camp.

The Camp Preparation Pennant shown here will be earned by a Patrol which can carry out the six parts of the Camp Preparation challenge without a hitch

Learning how to pitch a tent at summer camp

CAMP – a magic word for so many Guides. The chance to spend a whole thrilling week or more with one's friends, and experience the fun of life under canvas in the great outdoors.

A chance to put into full practice so many things a Guide may only have experimented with in the garden, park or playground. Pitching a tent that you are actually going to sleep in is far more exciting than merely putting one up to discover how to do it. There is, too, a definite art to rolling up camp bedding and stacking it neatly clear of the ground by day on a gadget you have made yourself. You then quickly discover if your woodcraft skill in selecting wood and lashing the parts together is up to standard – or not! Gadgets which look so sturdy, strong and neat when you first erect them, often have a nasty habit of collapsing under the weight of a roll of bedding! But it's all part of the fun, and everyone learns quickly from their mistakes!

Rolling up bedding to stack above ground during the day

A camp kitchen is very different from the kitchen at home, and offers many more opportunities for amusing 'disasters.' Even a stew which has 'caught' on the bottom of the dixie, and potatoes you yourself have peeled, nicking your fingers at the same time, can taste quite different and surprisingly good when cooked over a camp-kitchen fire or stove. Appetites become so enormous in the open-air life that there is no place for finickiness over food.

A typical camp kitchen

A beach fire at sunset

At camp a Guide can discover the beauty and wonder of the stars, perhaps for the first time in her life. She can take part in Wide Games. These are games covering a wide area of land, perhaps involving tracking skills. She may put into practical use her knowledge of map reading, or following compass directions, perhaps to find a hidden treasure, or by strategy to capture another Patrol's stronghold.

She might have a chance to visit a local farm, and make friends with the animals, and learn something of the busy life of the farmer, and his wife, and helpers.

The highlight of camp life is always the Camp Fire Entertainments and Sing Song in the evenings. It's a joy to sing Guide and Scout songs at any time, but to sit round a big blazing fire, in the cool of the evening, perhaps with the glorious smell of potatoes baking in their jackets among the embers, is so enjoyable that no words can describe it.

The Guides have a special hymn they sing at the close of all Guiding events. It is called TAPS. This word originally came from the tapping on a drum which, in the American army, was the signal to retire. Later it became a bugle call, but still kept its name. To hear this sung around the dying embers of a Camp Fire last thing at night is an experience few Guides, or visitors, ever forget. Its words have special significance and meaning in such a setting:

Day is done,
Gone the sun,
From the sea,
From the hills,
From the sky.
All is well,
Safely rest,
God is nigh.

Yes, 'God is nigh,' and this is a fact Guides have before them throughout their years of Guiding. 'I promise to do my duty to God' is the first clause of the Promise the Guide makes, and in saying this she is putting God in His rightful place – *first* in her life.

Many Guide Companies attend a religious service once a month with their local Youth Organisations, and a Guide finds this a help in getting to know more about God and discovering how best she can serve Him.

Guides hold a Christmas carol service

One way in which a Guide serves God is by developing the skills He has given her, and using them to help others.

The idea of service begins in Brownie Guides, when a new member at her Brownie Promise Ceremony recites the Brownie Law. This Law is, 'A Brownie Guide thinks of others before herself and does a Good Turn every day.' When she becomes a Guide she is expected to do *at least* one Good Turn every day, but whereas a Brownie may be encouraged to

record and talk about her Good Turns with the Guider in charge, so developing a good habit, a Guide does not talk about her good turns. She just does them as quietly and efficiently as she can, without thought of any reward. Maybe the good turn will be a simple small one, like noticing if someone is following her through a door and holding it open for them instead of letting it slam back in their face; or it

A new Brownie

may be a more spectacular good turn such as pulling a child out of a river. Both are good turns, the first depending on the development of thoughtfulness and consideration for others, the second on the development of quick thinking and physical skill.

A Guide helping Brownies to prepare for a party

Ranger Guides helping at an old people's home

A Guide may stay in the Guide Company until she is fifteen, but between the ages of fourteen and fifteen she may go on into a Ranger Guide Unit if there is one in her District. There she will find that new activities and fresh adventures await her, but in a more grown-up setting. A Ranger Guide at her investiture affirms that her special responsibility as a Ranger is to be of service in the community. She is now Looking Wider as the Founder of the Movement, Robert Baden-Powell, said all Guides and Scouts were to do.

In the Ranger Guide Unit she will have opportunities to develop the skills she has learnt in the Guide Company to a higher level: skills in First Aid

and Home Nursing, Housecraft and Child Care, Creative Crafts and Physical Abilities. She will have opportunities for greater adventures, perhaps exploring the countryside on horseback, discovering the thrills of canoeing, or the exhilaration of mountain and rock climbing. She will have the companionship of camping and other social events with Venture Scouts, visiting Rangers in other countries, learning to service and fly a plane, sail a boat, service a car, ski proficiently.

But holding together all the interesting, exciting adventures, and worthwhile things a Guide or Ranger Guide does, is the Promise. The foundation of all Guiding and Scouting.

Index

	page
Age limits	4, 50
American Girl Scouts	12, 13
Baden-Powell, Lady Olave	13
Baden-Powell, Lord Robert	
	8-10, 12, 13, 23, 50
Badges:	
Eight Point	34, 35
Interest	24, 32, 36
Promise	17, 34
Service	37
Brownie Guides	4, 8, 48, 49
Camping	5, 40-44, 51
Collecting schemes	24, 25, 33
Company Funds	22, 24
Creative crafts	7, 24, 27, 28, 31
Eight Point Programme	34, 53
Exploring	4
First aid	6, 50
Friendship Fund	26
Games	4, 44
Handbook	29, 36
Historic buildings	4, 6
Law	16
Low, Juliette	12
Map reading	4, 7, 31
Motto	14, 18

	page
New members	18, 19
Patrol Emblems	20, 34
Patrol Interest Pennants	38, 39
Patrol Leader	21
Pen-friends	7
Promise	4, 14, 15, 34, 45, 51
Ranger Guides	50-51
Scouting	4, 8
Singing	44
Swimming	4, 6
Taps	44, 45
Tracking	4, 5, 44
Woodcraft	39, 41
World Association	13, 14